Diamond and herringbone pattern gansey being worn by John West (left), a lifeboatman who, with Tony Crask (right), as Sheringham Methodist Evangelists, travelled the country preaching.

FRONT COVER: Three Sheringham fishermen, about 1910: (from left to right) John 'Tarr' Bishop, Elijah Farrow and Belcher Johnson.

FISHERMAN KNITTING

Michael Harvey and Rae Compton

Shire Publications Ltd

CONTENTS

Introduction   3
Social and economic importance   5
Knitting sheaths   1 1
The decline of traditional
    fisherman knitting   1 2
Pullovers for fishermen   1 3
Fishermen's coloured garments   1 5

Knitting instructions

Cabled gansey   1 8
V-neck Fair Isle sweater   2 1
Fisherman's yoked sweater   2 4
Aran sweater with round or
    polo neck   2 7

Printed in Great Britain by C. I. Thomas & Sons (Haverfordwest) Ltd, Press Buildings, Merlins Bridge, Haverfordwest, Dyfed.

ACKNOWLEDGEMENTS

The authors wish to thank Patons and Baldwins for supplying the instructions for the Fair Isle garment and arranging the check knitting of all the designs in this book, which have been produced using their yarns, Nan Govan for her advice with the project, Alan Gillard for providing reproducible photographs, and Edna Gambie for typing the manuscript from a barely decipherable original. Photographs are acknowledged as follows: L. West, page 1; D.C. Higgins, page 5; Mrs Mason, pages 7 (top left), 12, front cover; Lowestoft Library, page 13; Thomson Newspapers Ltd, page 17 (top right); C. Goffin, pages 4 (bottom), 17 (top left).

Fishermen wearing traditionally patterned ganseys posing in the old stocks at Southwold in 1901.

Men, wearing knitted pullovers, making herring barrels, while two women, wearing knitted shawls, stand by knitting.

INTRODUCTION

The craft of hand knitting dates back to before the time of Christ: the earliest recorded form of knitting originated in the Middle East. Different forms of the craft developed at later dates in other parts of the world: for example, Peruvian needle knitting and Scandinavian forms referred to as *sprang*. The Coptic Christians brought knitting from the Mediterranean region to Europe and to England, from where it spread round the coast to Scotland, Wales and Ireland.

In the British Isles knitting was carried out in the home in its early days, but in the later middle ages it became an industry organised by guilds, whose master knitters controlled quality and levels of production. During the reign of Elizabeth I the Reverend William Lee developed a knitting machine, which eventually ousted hand knitting as gainful employment in all but a few rural and coastal areas. If it were not for the strong traditions of knitting that had developed within these areas, the craft could easily have disappeared entirely owing to the relative cheapness of machine-knitted garments, and perhaps the resurrection of hand knitting as a pastime during the nineteenth century would never have occurred. This book is about one particular area of knitting which contains elements of the social, economic and aesthetic byways of the craft: that is, the tradition of knitting the fisherman's jersey-type garment — the Aran and gansey knitting, which became an art form.

Instructions are provided which will enable some types of these fishermen's garments to be re-created in the modern idiom whilst at the same time retaining their traditional form.

3

James Haylett, photographed in the early 1900s aged seventy-eight, wearing a typical hand-knitted gansey. Formerly second coxswain of the lifeboat 'Beauchamp', he is wearing the medal of the Lifeboat Institution presented to him by Edward VII at Sandringham.

William George Larner wearing the traditional sealskin cap and gansey hand-knitted in the Larner pattern, about 1880. The eleven rings on the sleeves may denote the number of his children.

4

Caister lifeboatmen about 1906 or 1907: (from left, back row) John Plummer, Frank Clowes, Solomon Brown; (front row) John Haylett, James Haylett, Walter Haylett. Solomon Brown is wearing a gansey with the rare flowerpot pattern.

SOCIAL AND ECONOMIC IMPORTANCE

Fishermen's knitted garments have a beauty of their own, deriving from the intricate stitches which build up into fine patterns on a dark blue or cream background, or from the use of bright colours according to the various traditions of the garments.

Quite often the knitted garment was the fisherman's main upper top garment, although in some places a navy slop would be worn over it. Collars and ties were rarely worn by fishermen. The fisherman's best garment was preserved very carefully for special occasions such as Sundays and saint's days and was frequently worn at his wedding, since years ago people did not possess suits.

Although photographs of fishermen at work invariably show them wearing their slops over their woollies, many photographs, especially family ones, show them at leisure, proudly wearing their knitted garments, which would normally have been made for them by their wives. A number of photographs show fishermen wearing scarves within the neck of their ganseys, although expert knitters made them fit so tightly that scarves were not necessary.

These garments soon developed implications of social significance. Firstly, because they were the product of a close-knit community, they helped to bring its people even closer together. On fine days the women of the fishing community would gather in groups on the beach to do their knitting together, chatting to each other and perhaps waiting for their husbands to return from their work at sea. On colder, darker nights they

would meet at each other's houses, gossiping while they knitted by the light of rush and tallow candles or paraffin lamps. There would have been considerable rivalry amongst the women, with each knitter being convinced that she knitted the finest garment for miles around, while the men proudly showed off the latest ones.

Ganseys developed another socially significant aspect: they were knitted in elaborate patterns which identified the wearer's family or village. They indicated social status and became the fisherman's 'coat of arms'. Because individual families kept the same patterns for their garments and the village had a few distinctive designs for the members of its community, and through the development of area traditions, the fisherman's garment became a symbol of belonging. Therefore many ports and areas developed traditional combinations of stitch patterns for their different fishing fleets. Stitch patterns such as anchor, cables, diamonds, flag, hailstone, herringbone, lightning, moss stitch, rope-ladder and shell would be combined in significant ways for different families and villages. The stitch patterns themselves were often the knitter's interpretation of things significant in the fisherman's life – his tools, harvest and the weather.

In the Cornish ports, when a young fisherman courted his future bride, she would knit him an elaborately patterned jersey. This was to be worn on their wedding day and was referred to as a *bridal shirt*. The pattern on the garment would be a traditional combination of stitches of the couple's village. Thus at annual fairs and on other occasions when the garment was worn, the pattern enabled an onlooker

John 'Tarr' Bishop photographed about 1900 wearing a gansey with a herringbone stitch pattern.

6

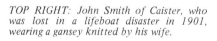

TOP RIGHT: John Smith of Caister, who was lost in a lifeboat disaster in 1901, wearing a gansey knitted by his wife.

ABOVE: This is the only machine-made gansey shown in this book. It is being worn by Squinter West, a Sheringham fisherman and lifeboatman, about 1890. The use of knitting machines led to the decline in the craft of hand-knitting ganseys.

RIGHT: Sid Jarvis of Southwold photographed in the early 1960s wearing a gansey that was hand-knitted in the flat.

7

LEFT: Henry Christopher Middleton with his wife and daughter, about 1920. Mrs Middleton knitted the gansey her husband is wearing.

RIGHT: Two Southwold fishermen wearing ganseys typical of the port, about 1900. These two men, Jack Sagine and Bunny Simpson, fished from Scottish boats for a time and are wearing Tam o' Shanters.

to distinguish from which village each man came.

It is said that these pattern combinations had another, more macabre use. If a fisherman was lost overboard and his body was not recovered but drifted down the coast with the tide, as long as he was wearing his traditional gansey the people who found him could identify his home village. A message would then be sent to the village that one of their menfolk had been found. Thus, as well as aesthetic and social qualities, traditional patterned ganseys had practical uses: warmth and comfort for the living, and identification of the dead; so they contributed to the efficiency and the economy of coastal villages.

The economic influence of fisherman knitting was considerable. The gansey was an indispensable tool of the fisherman's trade, for he needed a garment which gave him warmth and protection, yet at the same time allowed him freedom of movement and comfort, and the knitted garments were designed to provide both. Exposed to the elements, fishermen faced extremes of climate when working both on shore and at sea. They appreciated the comfort and protective qualities of a woollen jersey which, because of the closeness of the knit, was waterproof as well as giving protection from biting winds.

Ganseys also had a direct economic significance. People would knit them for those who could afford to pay a few shillings for a garment. Some fishermen had to buy them because there was no immediate member of their family to make them. Such knitting for profit was generally done on a small scale and did not offer much reward for what was an arduous and painstaking task. However, the payments were quite often a very necessary part of the family income. Where there was a large port nearby, the knitting of garments for sale to fishermen developed on a larger scale. There was much coming and going, and the deep-sea fishermen using the port provided a market for the garments.

Inevitably some garments were produced by the 'putting out' system, and knitting became a thriving cottage industry. Some knitters made small items such as ski hats and mitts as well as the jersey-type garments. Hand knitting was sometimes carried out in a factory as well as in the home, although the workers employed in the factory were probably mainly finishing off machine-made garments.

Ganseys took two weeks to make, and the knitter had to work quite hard to complete a garment in this time. Around the 1900s the pay was about 3s 6d (17½p) for each garment completed.

8

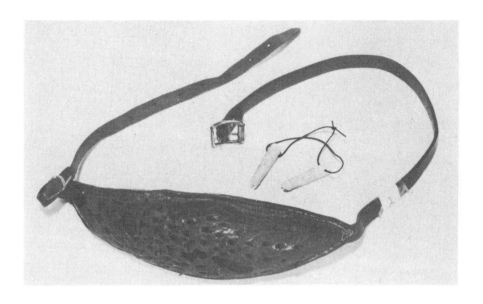

A leather sheath and carved bone stoppers from the collection of Michael Harvey.

Mrs Amando Goffin knitting at Winterton in 1964. She is knitting in the round and using a sheath.

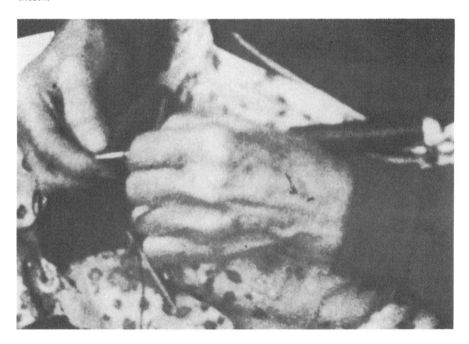

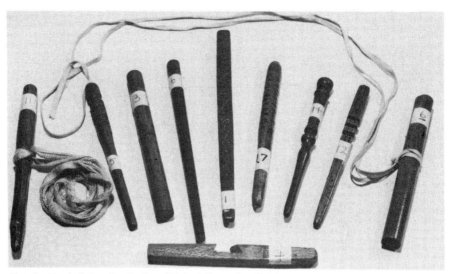

East Anglian knitting sheaths from Michael Harvey's collection.

KNITTING SHEATHS

Many knitters used knitting sheaths (which have also been referred to as knitting sticks, knitting bodkins or knitting shields). These have been written about widely, especially in connection with the Yorkshire Dales, where frequent reference is made to lovers carving them as tokens of esteem for their betrothed or loved ones. Knitting sheaths were widely used in many parts of the continent as well as in the British Isles. There are a number of variants, as well as some cruder methods of fulfilling the same function, which basically is to support the static needle holding the work, thus taking part of its weight and enabling the knitter to work more easily and quickly and with less effort. Rolled-up sailcloth and bundles of straw tied with tape were sometimes used: the needle was stuck into these for support. The leather pouch type with its belt seems to have been used only in Scotland or places with Scottish influence. Usually, though, support was provided using a short piece of

wood some 6 inches (15 cm) long with a hole, into which the needle was inserted, bored in the end. The piece of wood was generally stuck into a belt or tied round the waist with tape to give support, although some examples have a groove which clipped on to the belt instead.

The wood for carving the sheaths sometimes came from an old boat, and they were often made by a loved one or relative. Some were square in shape, others were turned; they might be carved or figured by scorching. Occasionally the initials of the prospective owner were added. Such sheaths were invariably made to be used. Although in many cases they eventually became treasured possessions they were rarely originally or entirely made with any thought of special affection, such as to provide a love token. Any sentimental connotation became attached to them later. In some areas there was a market in sheaths as a number of firms machine-produced them for sale.

11

A group of fishermen wearing traditional ganseys, about 1900. From left to right: Bobhot Cooper, Obadiah Cooper, Baker Grice, George Farrow.

THE DECLINE OF TRADITIONAL FISHERMAN KNITTING

As with most rural crafts, the advent of industrialisation caused the decline of the hand knitting of fishermen's garments, since machine-made ones were cheaper. Perhaps this change took longer with fishermen's garments because many of the smaller ports were situated away from the areas which became industrialised during the nineteenth century; they were rather isolated and demand was not great. Even with the coming of the railways, trips from these areas to the large towns or cities were rare.

It was not until after the First World War, when motor transport enabled more visitors to reach remote areas, that the old traditions began to crumble rapidly away. By the early twentieth century fishermen's garments were being machine-made for sale in the larger ports. While the older fishermen still looked upon the hosiery (machine-made) garment as inferior, it was soon realised that the womenfolk could spend their time more profitably than in knitting ganseys and the younger men were soon converted to wearing the machine-made ones. At the same time the older generation of fishermen was not being replaced, as the sons of families with long fishing traditions were no longer making their living from the sea.

So the mothers had no need to pass their skills on to their daughters. Thus today it is rare to find anyone who knits these fishermen's garments in the traditional manner. However, during various periods, the fishermen's designs have been popularised. In the following pages the major groupings of fishermen's garments will be discussed and instructions given for knitting some of them.

PULLOVERS FOR FISHERMEN

Many different traditions developed in the production of pullovers for fishermen. However, they all had two basic characteristics: they provided warmth and kept out the wind and rain, and they adopted distinctive patterns, sometimes bright as in the case of Fair Isle, Shetland and Scandinavian garments, and sometimes beautifully patterned in a single colour such as in Aran and gansey knitting. Exceedingly good examples of knitting traditions were found amongst knitters on small islands and in the fishing communities in coastal strips.

One of the finest developments in fisherman knitting was that of the gansey, which was the main type of port sweater found amongst the fishermen in England and Scotland. The word can be written as either *gansey* or *guernsey*. The *English Dialect Dictionary* (Oxford, 1900) states that the word *gansey* is used in Yorkshire, the Shetland Isles and Suffolk, although in east Suffolk it is also written as *ganzy*. Basically a gansey is a thick, closely fitted upper garment

An undated picture postcard entitled 'Herring Lasses Off Duty'.

13

which has been knitted in the round, generally in blue wool, and worn by fishermen as a jersey. Note the use of the names of the two Channel Islands, Jersey and Guernsey, for such pullover-type garments. When hand-knitted in a wool of about 3 or 4 ply thickness using very fine needles (which frequently produce a fabric with a stitch count of 12 stitches and 20 rows to the inch), the garment produced combines warmth with comfort and freedom of movement.

MAKING A GANSEY

Most present-day knitters, even skilled ones, will probably doubt their ability to knit a gansey in the traditional manner. But although it may seem to be a work of art, before the machine desecrated the craft hand knitters took the task in their stride.

Owing to the development of such a large variety of designs, there were differences in how they were made, but the following general description of how they were made in East Anglia shows the basic concept.

The yarn used was a heavy woollen one which was worsted spun in about 4 ply thickness; it was traditionally a dark navy colour, which was not adversely affected by salt water, and is called abb wool (often pronounced *hob*).

The traditional gansey would be knitted in the round. The number of needles used depended upon their length, with anything from four 14 inch (35 cm) ones to ten or eleven 6 inch (15 cm) ones, and they varied in size from 14s to 17s. Invariably the knitter supported her needle by using a knitting sheath.

The stitch had to be fine and the garment tightly knitted to keep out the wind. Surprisingly, this did not make the garment board-like, as tightly knitted fabrics can be. The number of stitches used would depend upon the size of the garment, but was frequently reckoned by the score, with 18 to 20 score on average. The amount of yarn going into the garment also

depended upon its size and the thickness of the yarn used and was from 24 ounces to 32 ounces (700 to 900 grams).

Casting on in the round at the bottom, the rib was knitted from 2 to 4 inches (5 to 10 cm) long, and the garment would then be continued in stocking stitch (patterns will be dealt with later) up to just under the arms, where the garment was opened up on both its sides, and then continued for its required length. It would be joined at the top in rib and the neck finished off in the round. The stitches at the sides of the armholes would be picked up and knitted downwards, finally being completed in the rib for the cuffs! There was no sewing at all. The sleeves would never be knitted too long, as can be seen from many of the photographs, to allow for freedom of movement and to keep the cuffs out of water. There were no written instructions but the knitter was generally able to decide how many stitches to put on by looking at the person who was going to wear the garment. Some fishermen preferred plain garments, others all-over patterns. However, most liked the bottom half of the garment to be plain with some pattern on the top half. The sleeves, or at least their bottom halves, were preferred plain. The plain and the patterned parts of the garment were separated by ridges.

Ganseys took anything from just under a week to six weeks to complete. Knitters working in the domestic industry tended to complete at least two ganseys a month.

The instructions for ganseys were handed down verbally from mother to daughter. The men were proud of their ganseys and never wore a shabby one. Because of the method by which they were knitted it was easy to repair them and in time each part of a gansey was likely to have been replaced, so that in extreme cases none of the original remained. If the cuffs, welt or neck became ragged, they would be taken out and replaced, or a whole sleeve would be re-knitted if necessary.

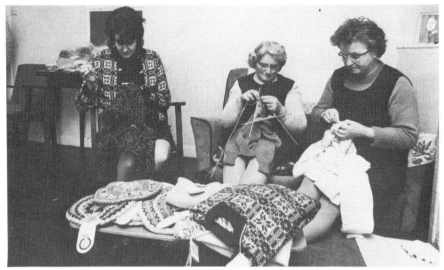

Three ladies of the Westray Knitters Society Limited. This co-operative has fifty members amongst the 740 inhabitants of the small Orkney isle of Westray.

FISHERMEN'S COLOURED GARMENTS

FAIR ISLE

The Fair Isle tradition derives its name from a small island that lies off the Shetland Isles. In 1588, about the time that the knitting machine was invented, one of the vessels from the shattered Spanish Armada was wrecked off the island and it is said that the inhabitants copied their knitting patterns from the clothes worn by the Spanish sailors. These patterns include the Armada Cross, the Rose of Sharon and various symbolic representations of the stars.

In knitting a Fair Isle garment, the colour of the wool used as a ground for the bands going across it is constantly changed.

It was common practice in Fair Isle for a grandmother to knit her grandson his first Fair Isle sweater to be worn when he reached adolescence. This was referred to as a Robe of Glory. Each pattern used in the sweater would be significant, usually commencing with the Water of Life and continuing with the Seed of Life,

the Anchor of Hope and Stars to guide him on his way. The pattern concluded at the shoulders with a Crown of Glory, to be the wearer's final reward if he led a good life.

Towards the end of the First World War, sailors of the United States Navy stationed in the area did much to popularise Fair Isle garments by sending them to friends in England and America, and in the 1920s the Prince of Wales (later King Edward VIII and then Duke of Windsor) wore them, thus adding to their popularity. Since then designs have been widely copied and adapted.

It is a common mistake to refer to any example of coloured pattern work as 'Fair Isle'. Genuine Fair Isle is always knitted with a ground of white, fawn, grey or brown, using bright colours for the patterning on this ground. It is knitted in with a wide pattern band using many colours, followed by a narrower band of only one or two colours. These pattern bands in true Fair Isle knitting vary all the way up the jersey, no two being exactly the same.

SHETLAND KNITTING

Shetland knitting is quite distinct from Fair Isle: much Shetland knitting has a basic all-over design. Although in traditional Shetland knitting the bands of pattern are of the same width, the patterns themselves are different. One band will have a light ground and dark pattern and the next a dark ground and light pattern and so on. The colours used are much more subdued than those found in Fair Isle knitting. Also, in Shetland knitting, the ribs are worked with a plain stitch in one colour and purl in another, a method not found in other fisherman knitting. The genuine Shetland garment is produced using Shetland wool which has been carded, spun and dyed with natural vegetable dyes. This hand-spun wool is unique in its appearance and has a soft, warm feel. The fineness of the wool is the direct result of the meagre grazing provided for Shetland sheep, which are kept on hill pastures throughout the year as the richer pastures of the valleys would cause the fibres to become coarse. Shetland wool was traditionally roved from the sheep, that is plucked by hand – a painless process as it comes away at the touch.

The traditions of the Shetland patterns derive from Scandinavia for in the ninth and tenth centuries the island was settled by immigrants from Norway, who strongly influenced their new homeland.

SCANDINAVIAN KNITTING

The traditional fisherman's garment worn by the Scandinavian fishermen was brightly coloured: coloured knitting has been the speciality of this part of the world for centuries. Using a white ground, darker colours such as dark green, dull red and navy are used to form the pattern. Fishermen's garments tended to have symmetrical patterns, sometimes with large, squarish-style designs, but garments with smaller all-over patterns can also be found. In recent years the designs for popular consumption have become more complicated and take motif form.

Danish knitting follows the same tendencies and, as the Faroes are influenced by the Danes, their fisherfolk have patterns on their garments quite distinct from those of the Fair Isle or Shetland fishermen. Again, garments are mainly knitted using colours, this time brighter than the traditional dull hues used in Scandinavian knitting.

ARAN

Off the coast of Ireland near Galway Bay lie the Aran Isles (not to be confused with the Isle of Arran in the Firth of Clyde off the coast of Scotland). There the fishermen wear a sweater, knitted in plain cream, which is heavily patterned, the style of which has become one of the best known in knitting – Aran. The patterns, although having the distinctive Aran look, are not local but are based on families. A design of heavily embossed cable and trellis-type patterns gives the garment a rugged look which is most appropriate for fishermen's wear. The pattern covers the complete garment – front, back and sleeves. The tradition is that families show their links through the patterns on the sweaters, and you can tell the strength of the connection and place in the family through a careful interpretation of the design. The stranger just about to join the family through marriage will have a garment composed mainly of stocking stitch with a small patterned panel up the centre. On the birth of a son, the basic panel will be retained but widened by adding a different pattern each side of it. The next son will have the same basic centre panel, but a different widening panel. Grandchildren will widen the centre panel still further. Thus family patterns are perpetuated and added to over time. The garments are referred to as *sea shirts* and it is suggested that some of their designs have been added to for more than two centuries (and so the family links in the sea shirt design go back many years).

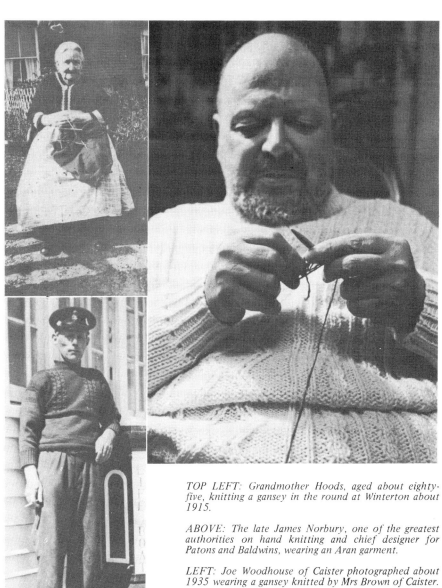

TOP LEFT: Grandmother Hoods, aged about eighty-five, knitting a gansey in the round at Winterton about 1915.

ABOVE: The late James Norbury, one of the greatest authorities on hand knitting and chief designer for Patons and Baldwins, wearing an Aran garment.

LEFT: Joe Woodhouse of Caister photographed about 1935 wearing a gansey knitted by Mrs Brown of Caister.

17

Cazey Goffin of Winterton-on-Sea wearing a cabled gansey that can be knitted from the instructions below.

KNITTING INSTRUCTIONS FOR CABLED GANSEY

Materials: 29[30, 32] (25 gram) balls *Patons Pure Wool Double Knitting* (Superwash).

Keep ball bands for washing and pressing instructions.

Set of four Nos. 2¾ mm and 3¼ mm Milward needles with points at both ends and 1 extra No. 2¾ mm and 3¼ mm Milward needle with points at both ends. Needle sizes quoted are metric: equivalent UK sizes are No. 12 for 2¾ mm and No. 10 for 3¼ mm. 2 stitch-holders. Cable needle.

Measurements: To fit chest 40[42, 44] in (102[107, 112] cm); length from top of shoulders, 25¼[25½, 25¾] in (64[65, 65] cm); sleeve seam, 19[19, 20] in (48[48, 51] cm).

Check your tension by casting on 12 sts on No. 3¼ mm needles. Work 16 rows in stocking stitch. Cast off. The square should measure 2 in (5 cm) each way.

Sizes
The figures in square brackets [ ] refer to the medium and large sizes.

This garment has been specially designed for the size range given and it is regretted that no adaptations are available.

18

Abbreviations

K = knit; P = purl; st = stitch; sL1K = slip stitch knitways; psso = pass slip stitch over; tog = together; tbl = through back of loops.

inc = increase by working into front and back of stitch; dec = decrease by working 2 stitches together.

alt = alternate; rep = repeat; patt = pattern; in = inches, cm = centimetres; mm = millimetres.

M1 = make 1 stitch by picking up horizontal loop lying before next stitch and working into back of it.

M2 = make 2 stitches by picking up horizontal loop lying before next stitch and K into front and back of it.

C5 = cable 5, slip next 2 sts on cable needle and leave at back of work, K3, then K2 from cable needle.

BODY

With No. 2¾ mm needles, cast on 312 [328, 344] sts and using spare needle to facilitate working, work in rounds as follows:

1st round: * K2, P2; rep from * to end of round. Rep 1st round 17 times more.

Work 1 round more in rib inc 1 st on both the 78th[82nd, 86th] st and the 234th[246th, 258th] st (314[330, 346] sts).

Change to No. 3¼ mm needles and work in *patt* as follows:

1st round: * K2, (these 2 sts are seam sts), (P2, K2) 1[2, 3] times, (P2, K5, P2, K2) twice, P2, K30, P2, K2, (P2, K5, P2, K2) 3 times, P2, K30, P2, (K2, P2, K5, P2) twice, (K2, P2) 1[2, 3] times *, rep from * to * once.

2nd round: * K2, (P2, K2) 1[2, 3] times, (P2, K5, P2, K2) twice, P2, K14, P2, K14, P2, K2, (P2, K5, P2, K2) 3 times, P2, K14, P2, K14, P2, (K2, P2, K5, P2) twice, (K2, P2) 1[2, 3] times *, rep from * to * once.

3rd round: * K2, (P2, K2) 1[2, 3] times, (P2, K5, P2, K2) twice, P2, K12, P2, K2, P2, K12, P2, K2, (P2, K5, P2, K2) 3 times, P2, K12, P2,
K2, P2, K12, P2, (K2, P2, K5, P2) twice, (K2, P2) 1[2, 3] times *, rep from * to * once.

4th round: * K2, (P2, K2) 1[2, 3] times, (P2, K5, P2, K2) twice, P2, K10, (P2, K2) twice, P2, K10, (P2, K2, P2, K5) 3 times, P2, K2, P2, K10, (P2, K2) twice, P2, K10, P2, (K2, P2, K5, P2) twice, (K2, P2) 1[2, 3] times *, rep from * to * once.

5th round: * K2, (P2, K2) 1[2, 3] times, (P2, C5, P2, K2) twice, P2, K8, (P2, K2) 3 times, P2, K8, P2, K2, (P2, C5, P2, K2) 3 times, P2, K8, (P2, K2) 3 times, P2, K8, P2, (K2, P2, C5, P2) twice, (K2, P2) 1[2, 3] times *, rep from * to * once.

6th round: * K2, (P2, K2) 1[2, 3] times, (P2, K5, P2, K2) twice, P2, K6, (P2, K2) 4 times, P2, K6, P2, K2, (P2, K5, P2, K2) 3 times, P2, K6, (P2, K2) 4 times, P2, K6, P2, (K2, P2, K5, P2) twice, (K2, P2) 1[2, 3] times *, rep from * to * once.

7th round: * K2, (P2, K2) 1[2, 3] times, (P2, K5, P2, K2) twice, P2, K4, (P2, K2) 5 times, P2, K4, P2, K2, (P2, K5, P2, K2) 3 times, P2, K4, (P2, K2) 5 times, P2, K4, P2 (K2, P2, K5, P2) twice, (K2, P2) 1[2, 3] times *, rep from * to * once.

8th round: * K2, (P2, K2) 1[2, 3] times, (P2, K5, P2, K2) twice, (P2, K2) 9 times, (P2, K5, P2, K2) 3 times, (P2, K2) 8 times, P2, (K2, P2, K5, P2) twice, (K2, P2) 1[2, 3] times *, rep from * to * once.

9th round: * K2, (P2, K2) 1[2, 3] times, (P2, K5, P2, K2) twice, P2, (P2, K2) 7 times, P4, (K2, P2, K5, P2) 3 times, P2, K2, (P2, K2) 7 times, P4, (K2, P2, K5, P2) twice, (K2, P2) 1[2, 3] times *, rep from * to * once.

10th round:	as 8th
11th round:	as 7th
12th round:	as 6th
13th round:	as 5th
14th round:	as 4th
15th round.	as 3rd
16th round:	as 2nd

These 16 rounds form patt.

Continue in patt until work measures 11 in (28 cm).

Shape gussets as follows:

1st round: K1, M2, K1, patt 155 [163, 171], K1, M2, K1, patt to end of round.

Keeping continuity of patt and working 4 gusset sts as K sts, work a further 5 rounds.

7th round: * K1, M1, K2, M1, K1, patt 155[163, 171] *, rep from * to * once.

Keeping continuity of patt and gusset sts K, work a further 5 rounds.

Keeping continuity of patt, continue inc in this way at each side of gussets on next and every following 6th round until there are 22 gusset sts. Work 4 rounds more.

Divide for armholes as follows:

1st row: work across 22 gusset sts, patt 155[163, 171], turn and leave remaining sts on a length of yarn.

2nd row: patt 155[163, 171], turn and leave remaining 22 gusset sts on a stitch-holder.

Keeping continuity of patt, work across these sts for Back until armhole measures 6¾[7, 7¼] in (17[18, 18] cm), ending with right side facing. Leave sts on a spare needle.

With right side facing, rejoin yarn to remaining sts and work Front as follows: K across 22 gusset sts, leave these sts on a stitch-holder, patt to end.

Work as for Back until 16 rows less than on Back have been worked to shoulders, thus ending with right side facing for next row.

Shape neck as follows:

1st row: patt 66[68, 70], turn and leave remaining sts on a length of yarn.

Keeping continuity of patt, dec 1 st at neck edge on next 6 rows, then on every following alt row until 58[60, 62] sts remain. Work 5 rows.

Place front shoulder 58[60, 62] sts against corresponding back shoulder sts and with right sides together, cast off or graft sts.

With right side facing, leave centre 23[27,31] sts on a length of yarn, rejoin yarn to remaining sts and complete to correspond with first side, reversing shapings.

NECKBAND
With right side facing and No. 3¼ mm needles, K across 39[43, 47] sts from back, *knit up* 19 sts down left side of neck, K across 23[27, 31] sts from front and *knit up* 19 sts up right side of neck (100[108, 116] sts).

Work 12 rounds in K2, P2 rib. Cast off evenly in rib.

SLEEVES
With right side facing and No. 3¼ mm needles, rejoin yarn to gusset sts and K across these 22 sts, *knit up* 110 [114, 118] sts evenly round armhole (132[136, 140] sts).

1st round: K22, P2, * K2, P2; rep from * to end of round. Rep 1st round 4 times more.

Next round: K1, sL1K, K1, psso, K16, K2tog, K1, P2, * K2, P2; rep from * to end.

Keeping continuity of rib, dec 1 st at each side of gusset on every 6th round until 4 gusset sts remain, ending with a dec round. Work 5 rounds.

Next round: K2togtbl, K2tog, P2, * K2, P2; rep from * to end of round.

Keeping first 2 sts for seam, continue in rib dec 1 st at each side of seam sts on every following 4th round until 72[76, 80] sts remain.

Work a few rows straight if necessary until Sleeve measures 17[17, 18] in (43[43, 46] cm).

Change to No. 2¾ mm needles and work in K2, P2 rib for 2 in (5 cm). Cast off evenly in rib.

With wrong side facing, press lightly following instructions on the ball band.

20

The author, Michael Harvey, wearing a V-necked Fair Isle sweater, which can be knitted following the instructions below.

KNITTING INSTRUCTIONS FOR V-NECK FAIR ISLE SWEATER

Materials: 3[3, 3] (50 gram) balls in Main Shade, 1[1, 1] (50 gram) ball in 1st Contrast, 3[3, 3] (50 gram) balls in 2nd Contrast, 3[3, 3] (50 gram) balls in 3rd Contrast, 2[2, 2] (50 gram) balls in 4th Contrast and 1[1, 1] (50 gram) ball in 5th Contrast Patons Fiona.

Keep ball bands for washing and pressing instructions.

Pair each of Nos. 3¾ mm and 4 mm Beehive or Milward Disc needles. Needle sizes quoted are metric: equivalent UK sizes are No. 10 for 3¼ mm and No. 8 for 4 mm.

Measurements: To fit chest 38[40, 42] in (97[102, 107] cm); length from top of shoulders, approx 25½ [26, 26½] in (65[66, 67] cm); sleeve seam, approx 18 in (46 cm) all sizes.

Check your tension by casting on 23 sts on No. 4 mm needles. Work 30 rows in stocking stitch. Cast off. The square should measure 4 in (10 cm) each way.

Patt tension: 13½ sts and 13 rows to 2 in (5 cm) measured over patt on No. 4 mm needles.

Sizes: The figures in square brackets [ ] refer to the medium and large sizes.

This garment has been specially designed for the size range given and it is regretted that no adaptations are available.

21

Abbreviations

K = knit; P = purl; st = stitch; tog = together; tbl = through back of loops.

inc = increase by working into front and back of stitch; dec = decrease by working 2 stitches together.

beg = beginning; alt = alternate; rep = repeat; patt = pattern; in = inches; cm = centimetres; mm = millimetres; MS = Main Shade.

M1 = make 1 stitch by picking up horizontal loop lying before next stitch and working into back of it.

Note: When working in patt from chart, strand colour not in use loosely across wrong side of work over not more than 3 sts at a time to keep fabric elastic. Read odd rows K from right to left and even rows P from left to right. Join in and break off colours as required.

BACK

With No. 3¼ mm needles and MS, cast on 123[131, 139] sts and work in K1, P1 rib for 3½ in (9 cm), rows on right side having a K1 at each end and ending with *wrong* side facing for next row.

Next row: Rib 3[7, 4], M1, (rib 9[9, 10], M1) 13 times, rib to end (137 [145, 153] sts).

Change to No. 4 mm needles and work rows 1 to 28 from chart, repeating the 8 patt sts 17[18, 19] times across and odd st as indicated.

Continue in patt until Back measures approx 16½ in (42 cm), ending with a 28th patt row.

Keeping continuity of patt, *shape armholes* by casting off 5 sts at beg of next 2 rows. **

Dec 1 st at each end of every row until 117[121, 125] sts remain. Work 1 row.

Now dec 1 st at each end of next and every alt row until 105[109, 113] sts remain. Work straight until armhole measures 9[9½, 10] in (23[24, 25] cm), ending with right side facing for next row.

Shape shoulders by casting off 8 sts at beg of next 6 rows, 8[9, 10] sts at beg of next 2 rows. Leave remaining 41[43, 45] sts on a spare needle.

FRONT

Work as for Back to **

Divide for neck as follows:

Next row – K2tog, patt 61[65, 69] sts, turn and leave remaining sts on a spare needle.

Continue on these 62[66, 70] sts for first side, dec 1 st at neck edge on every alt row, *at the same time* dec 1 st at armhole edge on next 4[6, 8] rows, then on every alt row until 44[45, 46] sts remain.

Continue dec 1 st at neck edge *only* on every alt row until 37[38, 39] sts remain, then on every 4th row until 32[33, 34] sts remain.

Work straight until Front matches Back to shoulder shaping, ending with right side facing for next row.

Shape shoulders by casting off 8 sts at beg of next and following 2 alt rows. Work 1 row. Cast off remaining 8[9, 10] sts.

With right side facing, slip centre st on a safety-pin, rejoin appropriate colours to remaining sts, patt to last 2 sts, K2tog.

Finish to correspond with first side, reversing shapings.

SLEEVES

With No. 3¼ mm needles and MS, cast on 55[61, 61] sts and work in rib as on Back for 3½ in (9 cm), ending with *wrong* side facing for next row.

Next row: Rib 5[3, 3], M1, (rib 5, M1) 9[11, 11] times, rib to end (65[73, 73] sts).

Change to No. 4 mm needles and starting with a 19th patt row, work in patt from chart repeating the 8 patt sts 8[9, 9] times across and odd st as indicated, shaping sides by inc 1 st at each end of 5th[7th, 5th] and every following 5th[6th, 5th] row until

22

there are 91[95, 99] sts, taking inc sts into patt.

Work straight until sleeve seam measures approx 18 in (46 cm), ending with a 28th patt row.

Keeping continuity of patt, *shape top* by casting off 5 sts at beg of next 2 rows, then dec 1 st at each end of next and every alt row until 39[39, 43] sts remain.

Now dec 1 st at each end of every row until 29 sts remain. Cast off.

MAKE-UP AND NECK BORDER
With wrong side of work facing, block each piece by pinning out round edges, and omitting ribbing, press following instructions on the ball band.

Use 30 in (76 cm) lengths of yarn and a large needle for make-up, making sure yarn keeps its original twist by turning needle clockwise between fingers and thumb after every few stitches.

Using a fine back-stitch seam, join right shoulder.

With right side facing, No. 3¼ mm needles and MS, start at top of left shoulder and *knit up* 60[64, 68] sts down left side of neck, K1 from safety-pin (mark this st with a coloured thread), *knit up* 60[64, 68] sts up right side of neck, K41[43, 45] sts from back dec 3 sts evenly (159 [169, 179] sts).

1st row: * P1, K1; rep from * to 2 sts before marked st, P2tog, P1, P2togtbl, ** K1, P1; rep from ** to end.

2nd row: K1, * P1, K1; rep from * to 2 sts before marked st, P2togtbl, K1, P2tog, K1, ** P1, K1; rep from ** to end.

Rep last 2 rows 3 times more. Cast off evenly in rib dec as before.

Using a flat seam for ribbing and a fine back-stitch seam for remainder, join left shoulder, Neck Border, side and sleeve seams. Insert Sleeves. Press seams.

CHART for V-NECK COLOUR PATTERNED SWEATER

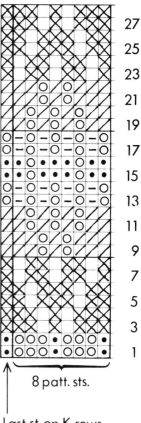

8 patt. sts.

Last st. on K rows

First st. on P rows

☐ MAIN SHADE

⊡ 1st CONTRAST

◯ 2nd CONTRAST

⊠ 3rd CONTRAST

⊘ 4th CONTRAST

⊟ 5th CONTRAST

Fisherman Leonard West in the yoked sweater for which knitting instructions are given below.

KNITTING INSTRUCTIONS FOR FISHERMAN'S YOKED SWEATER

Materials: 27[29, 31, 33] (25 gram) balls Patons Pure Wool Double Knitting (Superwash).

Keep ball bands for washing and pressing instructions.
Set of four Nos. 2 mm and 2¾ mm Milward needles with points at both ends and 1 extra No. 2 mm and No. 2¾ mm Milward needle with points at both ends. Needle sizes quoted are metric: equivalent UK sizes are No. 14 for 2 mm and No. 12 for 2¾ mm.

Measurements: To fit chest 38[40, 42, 44] in (97[102, 107, 112] cm); length, 26½[26½, 27, 27] in (67[67, 69, 69] cm); sleeve seam, 18[19, 19, 20] in (46[48, 48, 51] cm).

Check your tension by casting on 29 sts on No. 2¾ mm needles. Work 40 rows in stocking stitch. Cast off. The square should measure 4 in (10 cm) each way.

Sizes: The figures in square brackets [ ] refer to the 3 larger sizes.
   This garment has been specially designed for the size range given and it is regretted that no adaptations are available.

Abbreviations
K = knit; P = purl; st = stitch; tog = together; dec = decrease by working 2 stitches together.

rep = repeat; patt = pattern; in = inches; cm = centimetres; mm = millimetres.

M1 = make 1 stitch by picking up horizontal loop lying before next stitch and working into back of it.

24

M2 = make 2 stitches by picking up horizontal loop lying before next stitch and K into front and back of it.

Note: When working from chart read chart from * a-b; rep from b-c to within 6 sts of seam sts, work from c-d, P2; rep from * to end of round.

With No. 2 mm needles, cast on 268 [284, 300, 316] sts, and using spare needle to facilitate working, work in rounds of K2, P2 rib for 3 in (7 cm).

Change to No. 2¾ mm needles and work as follows:

1st round: * K132[140, 148, 156], P2; rep from * once.

The purl sts in this and following rounds mark the side 'seams'. Rep 1st round until work measures 13[13, 13½, 13½] in (33[33, 34, 34] cm).

Yoke: Now work in patt from chart and work 9[9, 5, 5] rounds.

Shape gusset as follows:

Next round: * Patt 132[140, 148, 156], P1, M2, P1; rep from * to end of round.

Work a further 5 rounds from chart working across seam sts as follows: P1, K2, P1.

Next round: * Patt 132[140, 148, 156], P1, M1, K2, M1, P1; rep from * to end of round.

Continue in patt from chart increasing 2 sts as before on each gusset on every following 6th round until there are 20 K sts on gusset. Work 5 rounds more.

Keeping continuity of patt, divide for *Front and Back* as follows:

** *1st row:* Patt 132[140, 148, 156], turn and leave remaining sts on a length of yarn.

Work a further 63[63, 67, 67] rows in patt, thus ending with a 66th row of patt. **

Shape front as follows:

1st row: K57[60, 63, 66], turn and leave remaining sts on a spare needle.

CHART for YOKED SWEATER

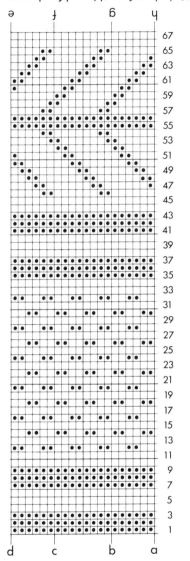

Work chart from 1–67 then repeat 1–67 once for body pattern

When working in rounds:—

☐ = KNIT STITCH   ▣ = PURL STITCH

25

2nd row: K2tog, K to end.
3rd row: P to last 2 sts, P2tog.
4th row: as 2nd.
5th row: K to last 2 sts, K2tog.
6th row: P2tog, P to end.
7th row: as 5th.
8th to 10th row: as 2nd to 4th.
11th row: K.
12th row: as 6th
13th row: K.
14th row: as 2nd.
15th row: P.
16th row: K.

Leave remaining 46[49, 52, 55] sts on a length of yarn.

With right side facing, leave centre 18[20, 22, 24] sts on a length of yarn, rejoin yarn to remaining sts and complete to correspond with first side, reversing shapings.

Back: With right side facing, leave next 22 sts on a length of yarn, rejoin yarn to remaining sts and work as for Front from ** to **.

Work a further 10 rows in patt.

Shape neck as follows:

1st row: K49[52, 55, 58] sts, turn and leave remaining sts on a length of yarn.
2nd row: P2tog, P to end.
3rd row: K to last 2 sts, K2tog.
4th row: K2tog, K to end.
5th row: P.
6th row: K.

Leave remaining 46[49, 52, 55] sts on a length of yarn.

With right side facing, leave centre 34[36, 38, 40] sts on length of yarn, rejoin yarn to remaining sts and complete to correspond with first side, reversing shapings.

With *wrong* sides together, graft back and front shoulder sts.

SLEEVES
With No. 2¾ mm needles, *knit up* 92[92, 100, 100] sts evenly around armhole, then P1, K20, P1 across gusset sts (114[114, 122, 122] sts).

Next 3 rounds: P to last 22 sts, P1,

K20, P1.

Next 2 rounds: K to last 22 sts, P1, K20, P1.

Next round: K to last 22 sts, P1, K2tog, K16, K2tog, P1.

Next 3 rounds: P to last 20 sts, P1, K18, P1.

Now work from chart reading chart from 67th round to 1st round and working sts as follows: Work from e-f; rep from f-g to within 6 sts of seam sts, work g-h, P1, K18, P1.

Keeping continuity of patt, continue dec 2 sts on gusset on every 6th round from previous dec until 94[94, 102, 102] sts remain.

Keeping 2 P sts for seam correct, continue in patt dec 1 st at each side of seam sts on every following 6th round until last round of patt has been worked (90[90, 98, 98] sts).

Now work in stocking stitch dec 1 st at each side of seam sts on every following 16th round from previous dec until 80[80, 88, 88] sts remain.

Work straight until Sleeve measures 15[16, 16, 17] in (38[41, 41, 43] cm).

Change to No. 2 mm needles and work in K2, P2 rib for 3 in (7 cm). Cast off evenly in rib.

NECKBAND
With right side facing and No. 2¾ mm needles, starting at left shoulder, *knit up* 18 sts down left side of neck, K18[20, 22, 24] sts from centre, *knit up* 18 sts up right side, 8 sts down right side of back, K34[36, 38, 40] from centre back, then *knit up* 8 sts up left side of back (104[108, 112, 116] sts).

Work in rounds of K2, P2 rib for 1½ in (4 cm). Cast off loosely in rib.

Fold Neckband in half to wrong side and slip-hem loosely in position.

With wrong side facing, press lightly following instructions on the ball band.

26

The Aran sweater here worn by John Symonds of Caister-on-Sea can be knitted from the instructions given below.

KNITTING INSTRUCTIONS FOR ARAN SWEATER WITH ROUND OR POLO NECK

Materials: Round Neck Version: 20 [22, 23] (50 gram) balls; *Polo Neck Version:* 21[23, 24] (50 gram) balls *Patons Capstan.*

Keep ball bands for washing and pressing instructions.

Pair each of Nos. 3¼ mm and 4 mm Beehive or Milward needles and set of four No. 3¼ mm Milward needles with points at both ends. Needle sizes quoted are metric: equivalent UK sizes are No. 10 for 3¼ mm and No. 8 for 4 mm. Beehive cable needle.

Measurements: To fit chest 40[42, 44] in (102[107, 112] cm); length from top of shoulders; 23½[24, 24½] in (60[61, 62] cm); sleeve seam, 18[19, 20] in (46[48, 51] cm).

Check your tension by casting on 10 sts on No. 4 mm needles. Work 13 rows in stocking stitch. Cast off. The square should measure 2 in (5 cm) each way.

Sizes

The figures in square brackets [ ] refer to the medium and large sizes.

This garment has been specially designed for the size range given and it is regretted that no adaptations are available.

Abbreviations

K = knit; P = purl; KB = knit into back of stitch; PB = purl into back of stitch; st = stitch; sL1K = slip stitch knitways; sL2P = slip 2 stitches purlways.

yfwd = yarn forward; kyb = keeping yarn back; kyft = keeping yarn front; psso = pass slipped stitch over; tog = together.

inc = increase by working into front and back of stitch; dec = decrease by working 2 stitches together.

beg = beginning; alt = alternate; rep = repeat; patt = pattern; in = inches; cm = centimetres; mm = millimetres.

M1K = make 1 knitways by picking up

loop that lies between st just worked and following st and *knitting* into back of it.

M1P = make 1 purlways by picking up loop that lies between st just worked and following st and *purling* into back of it.

C4F = slip next 2 sts on cable needle and leave at front of work, K2, then K2 from cable needle.

C4B = slip next 2 sts on cable needle and leave at back of work, K2, then K2 from cable needle.

C6 = slip next 2 sts on cable needle and leave at back of work, K next st, K2 from cable needle, slip next st on cable needle and leave at front of work, K2, then K st from cable needle.

Cr3 = Cross 3, slip next 2 sts on cable needle and leave at back of work, KB1, then P1, KB1 from cable needle.

Cr3R = slip next 2 sts on cable needle and leave at front of work, P next st, then KB2 from cable needle.

Cr3L = slip next st on cable needle and leave at back of work, KB2, then P st from cable needle.

Tw2F = Twist 2 Front by knitting into front of 2nd st, then front of first st on left-hand needle and slipping 2 sts off needle together.

Tw2B = Twist 2 Back by knitting into back of 2nd st, then back of first st on left-hand needle and slipping 2 sts off needle together.

MB = make bobble by (K1, yfwd, K1, yfwd, K1) all into next st, turn, P5, turn, K5, turn, P5, turn, sL1K, K1, psso, K1, K2tog, turn, P3tog, turn, keeping yarn at back slip bobble on to right-hand needle.

BACK
With No. 3¼ mm needles, cast on 102 [110, 117] sts.
1st size:
1st row: P1, K2, * P1, (KB1, P1) twice, K2; rep from * to last st, P1.

2nd row: K1, P2, * K1, (PB1, K1) twice, P2; rep from * to last st, K1.
3rd row: P1, K2, * P1, Cr3, P1, K2; rep from * to last st, P1.
4th row: as 2nd.
5th to 8th row: as 1st and 2nd twice.
9th row: as 3rd.
10th row: as 2nd.
11th to 14th row: as 1st and 2nd twice.
15th row: as 3rd.
16th row: as 2nd.
17th and 18th rows: as 1st and 2nd.
19th row: as 1st.

Increase row: Inc in first st, M1P, P1, M1P, P7, M1P, P1, K1, (P1, M1P) 3 times, K1, P1, M1P, P2, K3, P3, (K1, PB1) 3 times, K1, M1P, P2, K1, M1K, K2, M1K, K1, (PB1, K1) 3 times, M1P, P1, M1P, (P3, M1P) 3 times, P2, M1P, P1, M1P, P3, M1P, (K1, PB1) 3 times, M1K, K3, M1K, K1, P2, M1K, P1, (PB1, K1) 3 times, P3, K3, P2, M1P, P1, K1, (P1, M1P) 3 times, K1, P1, M1P, P7, M1P, P1, M1P, inc in last st (132 sts).

2nd and 3rd sizes:
1st row: * P1, (KB1, P1) twice, K2; rep from * to last 5 sts, (P1, KB1) twice, P1.

2nd row: * K1, (PB1, K1) twice, P2; rep from * to last 5 sts, (K1, PB1) twice, K1.

3rd row: * P1, Cr3, P1, K2; rep from * to last 5 sts, P1, Cr3, P1.
4th row: as 2nd.
5th to 8th row: as 1st and 2nd twice.
9th row: as 3rd.
10th row: as 2nd.
11th to 14th row: as 1st and 2nd twice.
15th row: as 3rd.
16th row: as 2nd.
17th and 18th rows: as 1st and 2nd.
19th row: as 1st.

2nd size:
Increase row: (P3, M1P) twice, P7, M1P, P1, K1, (P1, M1P) 3 times, K1, P1, M1P, P2, K3, P2, M1P, P1, (K1, PB1) 3 times, P2, M1P, P1, K1, M1K, K2, M1K, K1, (PB1, K1) 3 times, P1,

(M1P, P2) 7 times, M1P, P1, (K1, PB1) 3 times, K1, M1K, K2, M1K, K1, P1, M1P, P2, (PB1, K1) 3 times, P1, M1P, P2, K3, P2, M1P, P1, K1, (M1P, P1) 3 times, K1, P1, M1P, P7, (M1P, P3) twice, (140 sts).

3rd size:
Increase row: P1, M1P, P5, M1P, P7, M1P, P1, K1, (P1, M1P) 3 times, K1, P1, M1P, P2, K3, P2, M1P, P1, (K1, PB1) 3 times, P3, K1, M1K, K2, M1K, K1, M1K, (PB1, K1) 3 times, P1, M1P, (P3, M1P) 3 times, P2, M1P, P1, M1P, (P3, M1P) 3 times, P1, (K1, PB1) 3 times, M1P, K3, M1K, K1, P2, M1K, P1, (PB1, K1) 3 times, P1, M1P, P2, K3, P2, M1P, P1, K1, (P1, M1P) 3 times, K1, P1, M1P, P7, M1P, P5, M1P, P1 (148 sts).

All sizes:
Change to No. 4 mm needles and work in *patt* as follows:

1st row: K1, (Tw2F, Tw2B) 3[4, 4] times, P1, K2, kyb sL2P, K2, P1, K4, P1, MB, P1, K4, P1, Cr3, P1, KB1, P1, Cr3R, P3, MB, P2, KB1, P1, Cr3, P1, K24[24, 32], P1, Cr3, P1, KB1, P2, MB, P3, Cr3L, P1, KB1, P1, Cr3, P1, K4, P1, MB, P1, K4, P1, K2, kyb sL2P, K2, P1, (Tw2F, Tw2B) 3[4, 4] times, K1.

2nd row: P13[17, 17], K1, P2, kyft sL2P, P2, K1, P4, K3, P4, (K1, PB1) 3 times, K1, PB2, K7, (PB1, K1) 3 times, P24[24, 32], (K1, PB1) 3 times, K7, PB2, K1, (PB1, K1) 3 times, P4, K3, P4, K1, P2, kyft sL2P, P2, K1, P13[17, 17].

3rd row: K1, (Tw2B, Tw2F) 3[4, 4] times, P1, C6, P1, C4F, P3, C4B, (P1, KB1) 3 times, K1, Cr3L, P6, (KB1, P1) 3 times, (C4F, C4B) 3[3, 4] times, (P1, KB1) 3 times, P6, Cr3R, K1, (KB1, P1) 3 times, C4F, P3, C4B, P1, C6, P1, (Tw2B, Tw2F) 3[4, 4] times, K1.

4th row: P13[17, 17], K1, P6, K1, P4, K3, P4, (K1, PB1) 3 times, P1, K1, PB2, K6, (PB1, K1) 3 times, P24[24, 32], (K1, PB1) 3 times, K6, PB2, K1, P1, (PB1, K1) 3 times, P4, K3, P4, K1, P6, K1, P13[17, 17].

5th row: K1, (Tw2F, Tw2B) 3[4, 4] times, P1, K2, kyb sL2P, K2, P1, K4, P3, K4, (P1, KB1) 3 times, P1, K1, Cr3L, P5, (KB1, P1) 3 times, K24[24, 32], (P1, KB1) 3 times, P5, Cr3R, K1, P1, (KB1, P1) 3 times, K4, P3, K4, P1, K2, kyb sL2P, K2, P1, (Tw2F, Tw2B) 3[4, 4] times, K1.

6th row: P13[17, 17], K1, P2, kyft sL2P, P2, K1, P4, K3, P4, (K1, PB1) 3 times, K1, P1, K1, PB2, K5, (PB1, K1) 3 times, P24[24, 32], (K1, PB1) 3 times, K5, PB2, K1, P1, K1, (PB1, K1) 3 times, P4, K3, P4, K1, P2, kyft sL2P, P2, K1, P13[17, 17].

7th row: K1, (Tw2B, Tw2F) 3[4, 4] times, P1, C6, P1, C4B, P3, C4F, P1, Cr3, P1, KB1, K1, P1, K1, Cr3L, P4, KB1, P1, Cr3, P1, K24[24, 32], P1, Cr3, P1, KB1, P4, Cr3R, K1, P1, K1, KB1, P1, Cr3, P1, C4B, P3, C4F, P1, C6, P1, (Tw2B, Tw2F) 3[4, 4] times, K1.

8th row: P13[17, 17], K1, P6, K1, P4, K3, P4, (K1, PB1) 3 times, (P1, K1) twice, PB2, K4, (PB1, K1) 3 times, P24[24, 32], (K1, PB1) 3 times, K4, PB2, (K1, P1) twice, (PB1, K1) 3 times, P4, K3, P4, K1, P6, K1, P13[17, 17].

9th row: K1, (Tw2F, Tw2B) 3[4, 4] times, P1, K2, kyb sL2P, K2, P1, K4, P1, MB, P1, K4, (P1, KB1) 3 times, (P1, K1) twice, Cr3L, P3, (KB1, P1) 3 times, (C4B, C4F) 3[3, 4] times, (P1, KB1) 3 times, P3, Cr3R, (K1, P1) twice, (KB1, P1) 3 times, K4, P1, MB, P1, K4, P1, K2, kyb sL2P, K2, P1, (Tw2F, Tw2B) 3[4, 4] times, K1.

10th row: P13[17, 17], K1, P2, kyft sL2P, P2, K1, P4, K3, P4, (K1, PB1) 3 times, (K1, P1) twice, K1, PB2, K3, (PB1, K1) 3 times, P24[24, 32], (K1, PB1) 3 times, K3, PB2, (K1, P1) twice, K1, (PB1, K1) 3 times, P4, K3, P4, K1, P2, kyft sL2P, P2, K1, P13[17, 17].

11th row: K1, (Tw2B, Tw2F) 3[4, 4] times, P1, C6, P1, C4F, P3, C4B, (P1,

KB1) 3 times, (K1, P1) twice, K1, Cr3L, P2, (KB1, P1) 3 times, K24 [24, 32], (P1, KB1) 3 times, P2, Cr3R, (K1, P1) twice, K1, (KB1, P1) 3 times, C4F, P3, C4B, P1, C6, P1, (Tw2B, Tw2F) 3[4, 4] times, K1.

12th row: P13[17, 17], K1, P6, K1, P4, K3, P4, (K1, PB1) 3 times, (P1, K1) 3 times, PB2, K2, (PB1, K1) 3 times, P24[24, 32], (K1, PB1) 3 times, K2, PB2, (K1, P1) 3 times, (PB1, K1) 3 times, P4, K3, P4, K1, P6, K1, P13[17, 17].

13th row: K1, (Tw2F, Tw2B) 3[4, 4] times, P1, K2, kyb sL2P, K2, P1, K4, P3, K4, P1, Cr3, P1, KB1, (P1, K1) 3 times, Cr3L, P1, KB1, P1, Cr3, P1, K24[24, 32], P1, Cr3, P1, KB1, P1, Cr3R, (K1, P1) 3 times, KB1, P1, Cr3, P1, K4, P3, K4, P1, K2, kyb sL2P, K2, P1, (Tw2F, Tw2B) 3[4, 4] times, K1.

14th row: P13[17, 17], K1, P2, kyft sL2P, P2, K1, P4, K3, P4, (K1, PB1) 3 times, (K1, P1) 3 times, K1, PB2, K1, (PB1, K1) 3 times, P24[24, 32], (K1, PB1) 3 times, K1, PB2, K1, (P1, K1) 3 times, (PB1, K1) 3 times, P4, K3, P4, K1, P2, kyft sL2P, P2, K1, P13[17, 17].

15th row: K1, (Tw2B, Tw2F) 3[4, 4] times, P1, C6, P1, C4B, P3, C4F, (P1, KB1) 3 times, (K1, P1) 3 times, Cr3R, P1, (KB1, P1) 3 times, (C4F, C4B) 3[3, 4] times, (P1, KB1) 3 times, P1, Cr3L, (P1, K1) 3 times, (KB1, P1) 3 times, C4B, P3, C4F, P1, C6, P1, (Tw2B, Tw2F) 3[4, 4] times, K1.

16th row: P13[17, 17], K1, P6, K1, P4, K3, P4, (K1, PB1) 3 times, (P1, K1) 3 times, PB2, K2, (PB1, K1) 3 times, P24[24, 32], (K1, PB1) 3 times, K2, PB2, (K1, P1) 3 times, (PB1, K1) 3 times, P4, K3, P4, K1, P6, K1, P13[17, 17].

17th row: K1, (Tw2F, Tw2B) 3[4, 4] times, P1, K2, kyb sL2P, K2, P1, K4, P1, MB, P1, K4, (P1, KB1) 3 times, (P1, K1) twice, P1, Cr3R, P2, (KB1, P1) 3 times, K24[24, 32], (P1, KB1)

3 times, P2, Cr3L, (P1, K1) twice, P1, (KB1, P1) 3 times, K4, P1, MB, P1, K4, P1, K2, kyb sL2P, K2, P1, (Tw2F, Tw2B) 3[4, 4] times, K1.

18th row: P13[17, 17], K1, P2, kyft sL2P, P2, K1, P4, K3, P4, (K1, PB1) 3 times, (K1, P1) twice, K1, PB2, K3, (PB1, K1) 3 times, P24[24, 32], (K1, PB1) 3 times, K3, PB2, (K1, P1) twice, K1, (PB1, K1) 3 times, P4, K3, P4, K1, P2, kyft sL2P, P2, K1, P13 [17, 17].

19th row: K1, (Tw2B, Tw2F) 3[4, 4] times, P1, C6, P1, C4F, P3, C4B, P1, Cr3, P1, KB1, (K1, P1) twice, Cr3R, P3, KB1, P1, Cr3, P1, K24[24, 32], P1, Cr3, P1, KB1, P3, Cr3L, (P1, K1) twice, KB1, P1, Cr3, P1, C4F, P3, C4B, P1, C6, P1, (Tw2B, Tw2F) 3[4, 4] times, K1.

20th row: P13[17, 17], K1, P6, K1, P4, K3, P4, (K1, PB1) 3 times, (P1, K1) twice, PB2, K4, (PB1, K1) 3 times, P24[24, 32], (K1, PB1) 3 times, K4, PB2, (K1, P1) twice, (PB1, K1) 3 times, P4, K3, P4, K1, P6, K1, P13[17, 17].

21st row: K1, (Tw2F, Tw2B) 3[4, 4] times, P1, K2, kyb sL2P, K2, P1, K4, P3, K4, (P1, KB1) 3 times, P1, K1, P1, Cr3R, P4, (KB1, P1) 3 times, (C4B, C4F) 3[3, 4] times, (P1, KB1) 3 times, P4, Cr3L, P1, K1, P1, (KB1, P1) 3 times, K4, P3, K4, P1, K2, kyb sL2P, K2, P1, (Tw2F, Tw2B) 3[4, 4] times, K1.

22nd row: P13[17, 17], K1, P2, kyft sL2P, P2, K1, P4, K3, P4, (K1, PB1) 3 times, K1, P1, K1, PB2, K5, (PB1, K1) 3 times, P24[24, 32], (K1, PB1) 3 times, K5, PB2, K1, P1, K1, (PB1, K1) 3 times, P4, K3, P4, K1, P2, kyft sL2P, P2, K1, P13[17, 17].

23rd row: K1, (Tw2B, Tw2F) 3[4, 4] times, P1, C6, P1, C4B, P3, C4F, (P1, KB1) 3 times, K1, P1, Cr3R, P5, (KB1, P1) 3 times, K24[24, 32], (P1, KB1) 3 times, P5, Cr3L, P1, K1, (KB1, P1) 3 times, C4B, P3, C4F, P1, C6, P1, (Tw2B, Tw2F) 3[4, 4] times, K1.

24th row: P13[17, 17], K1, P6, K1, P4, K3, P4, (K1, PB1) 3 times, P1, K1, PB2, K6, (PB1, K1) 3 times, P24[24, 32], (K1, PB1) 3 times, K6, PB2, K1, P1, (PB1, K1) 3 times, P4, K3, P4, K1, P6, K1, P13[17, 17].

These 24 rows form patt.

Continue in patt until Back measures 16 in (41 cm), ending with right side facing for next row.

Keeping continuity of patt, *shape armholes* as follows: Cast off 3[4, 5] sts at beg of next 2 rows. Dec 1 st at each end of next 6 rows, then on next and every alt row until 106[106, 114] sts remain.

Work straight until armhole measures 7½[8, 8½] in (19[20, 21] cm), ending with right side facing for next row.

Shape shoulders as follows: Cast off 6[6, 7] sts at beg of next 2[2, 4] rows, then 6 sts at beg of next 8[8, 6] rows. Leave remaining 46[46, 50] sts on a length of yarn.

FRONT
Work as for Back until 16 rows less than on Back have been worked to start of shoulder shaping, ending with right side facing for next row.

Keeping continuity of patt, *shape neck* as follows:
Next row: Patt 40[40, 42] sts, turn and leave remaining sts on a length of yarn.

Continue on these sts for first side, dec 1 st at neck edge on next 5 rows, then on next and every alt row until 30[30, 32] sts remain. Work 1 row, thus ending with right side facing for next row.

Shape shoulder as follows: Cast off 6[6, 7] sts at beg of next and following alt row, then 6 sts at beg of following 2 alt rows. Work 1 row. Cast off remaining sts.

With right side facing, slip centre 26[26, 30] sts on a length of yarn, rejoin yarn to remaining sts and patt to end.

Complete as for first side, reversing shapings.

SLEEVES
With No. 3¼ mm needles, cast on 49[49, 56] sts.

1st row: * K1, (P1, KB1) twice, P1, K1; rep from * to end.

2nd row: * P1, (K1, PB1) twice, K1, P1; rep from * to end.

3rd row: * K1, P1, Cr3, P1, K1; rep from * to end.

4th row: as 2nd.
5th to 8th row: as 1st and 2nd twice.
9th row: as 3rd.
10th row: as 2nd.
11th to 14th row: as 1st and 2nd twice.
15th row: as 3rd.
16th row: as 2nd.
17th and 18th rows: as 1st and 2nd.
19th row: as 1st.

1st and 2nd sizes:
Increase row: P1, M1P, K1, PB1, M1P, K1, M1P, PB1, M1P, K1, P1, M1P, P1, K1, M1P, PB1, M1P, K1, PB1, M1P, K1, P1, M1P, P1, (K1, PB1) twice, K1, P1, M1P, P1, (K1, PB1) twice, K1, P1, M1P, P1, (K1, PB1) twice, K1, P1, M1P, P1, K1, M1P, PB1, K1, M1P, PB1, M1P, K1, P1, M1P, P1, K1, M1P, PB1, M1P, K1, M1P, PB1, K1, M1P, P1 (69 sts).

3rd size:
Increase row: P1, K1, M1P, PB1, K1, PB1, M1P, K1, M1P, P1, M1P, P1, K1, M1P, PB1, K1, M1P, PB1, M1P, K1, P1, M1P, P1, K1, M1P, (PB1, K1) twice, P1, M1P, P1, (K1, PB1) twice, K1, P1, M1P, P1, (K1, PB1) twice, K1, P1, M1P, P1, K1, M1P, PB1, K1, M1P, PB1, M1P, K1, P1, M1P, P1, K1, M1P, PB1, M1P, K1, PB1, M1P, K1, P1, M1P, P1, (K1, PB1) twice, M1P, K1, P1 (77 sts).

All sizes: Change to No. 4 mm needles and work in *patt* as follows:

1st row: K1, (Tw2F, Tw2B) 4[4, 5] times, P1, K2, kyb sL2P, K2, P1, Cr3, P1, K4, P1, MB, P1, K4, P1, Cr3, P1, K2, kyb sL2P, K2, P1, (Tw2F, Tw2B) 4[4, 5] times, K1.

2nd row: P17[17, 21], K1, P2, kyft sL2P, P2, (K1, PB1) twice, K1, P4, K3, P4, (K1, PB1) twice, K1, P2, kyft sL2P, P2, K1, P17[17, 21].

3rd row: K1, (Tw2B, Tw2F) 4[4, 5] times, P1, C6, (P1, KB1) twice, P1, C4F, P3, C4B, (P1, KB1) twice, P1, C6, P1, (Tw2B, Tw2F) 4[4, 5] times, K1.

4th row: P17[17, 21], K1, P6, (K1, PB1) twice, K1, P4, K3, P4, (K1, PB1) twice, K1, P6, K1, P17[17, 21].

5th row: K1, (Tw2F, Tw2B) 4[4, 5] times, P1, K2, kyb sL2P, K2, (P1, KB1) twice, P1, K4, P3, K4, (P1, KB1) twice, P1, K2, kyb sL2P, K2, P1, (Tw2F, Tw2B) 4[4, 5] times, K1.

6th row: P17[17, 21], K1, P2, kyft sL2P, P2, (K1, PB1) twice, K1, P4, K3, P4, (K1, PB1) twice, K1, P2, kyft sL2P, P2, K1, P17[17, 21].

7th row: K1, (Tw2B, Tw2F) 4[4, 5] times, P1, C6, P1, Cr3, P1, C4B, P3, C4F, P1, Cr3, P1, C6, P1, (Tw2B, Tw2F) 4[4, 5] times, K1.

8th row: P17[17, 21], K1, P6, (K1, PB1) twice, K1, P4, K3, P4, (K1, PB1) twice, K1, P6, K1, P17[17, 21].

Continue in patt, working appropriate cables as on Back, inc 1 st at each end of next and every following 6th row until there are 89[89,97] sts, taking extra sts into side patt.

Now inc 1 st at each end of every following 8th row until there are 97[97, 105] sts, taking inc sts into side patt as before.

Work straight until sleeve seam measures 18[19, 20] in (46[48, 51] cm), ending with right side facing for next row.

Keeping continuity of patt, *shape top* by casting off 3[4, 5] sts at beg of next 2 rows. Now dec 1 st at each end of next and every alt row until 71[57, 57] sts remain, then on every row until 29[31, 35] sts remain. Cast off.

MAKE-UP, NECK BORDER AND POLO NECK

With wrong side of work facing, block each piece by pinning out round edges, and omitting ribbing, press lightly following instructions on the ball band, taking care not to spoil the pattern.

Using a fine back-stitch seam, join shoulders.

With set of No. 3¼ mm needles, K across 46[46, 50] sts from back inc 4[4, 3] sts evenly, knit up 20 sts down side of neck, K across 26[26, 30] sts from front inc 3 sts evenly, knit up 20 sts up right side of neck (119[119, 126] sts).

1st round: * K1, (P1, KB1) twice, P1, K1; rep from * to end. Rep 1st round once more.

3rd round: * K1, P1, Cr3, P1, K1; rep from * to end.

4th to 8th round: As 1st.

Rep 3rd to 8th round until rib measures 2½ in (6 cm) for Round Neck or 6½ in (17 cm) for Polo Neck. Cast off loosely.

Fold in half to wrong side and slip-hem loosely in position.

Using a flat seam for ribbing and a fine back-stitch seam for remainder, join side and sleeve seams. Insert Sleeves.

Press seams.

FURTHER READING

Harvey, Michael. 'The Lore of the Norfolk Gansey'. *Norfolk Fair*, Sept. 1967.
Harvey, Michael. 'The Lore of the Suffolk Gansey'. *Suffolk Fair*, November 1972.
Jersey Island Federation of Women's Institutes. *Jerseys Old and New*. 1978.
Norbury, James. 'Traditional Knitted Sweaters'. *Centuries of Wool*, IWS.
Norbury, James. *Traditional Knitting Patterns*. Batsford, 1962.
Thompson, Gladys. *Guernsey and Jersey Patterns*. Batsford, 1955.
Tyne and Wear County Council Museums. *North East Fisher Ganseys*. 1977.